TRACK & FIELD
THE THROWS

MORGAN HUGHES

The Rourke Press, Inc.
Vero Beach, Florida 32964

Morgan Hughes is a sports writer who has covered professional hockey, baseball, tennis and cycling. He has written several childrens books, both fiction and nonfiction, and is currently at work on his first full-length novel.

PROJECT ADVISOR:
Richard Roberts is the former head track and field coach at Florida State University, where he was also a star athlete during his undergraduate studies. He resides in Tallahassee with his wife and three hunting dogs.

PHOTO CREDITS:
All photos by Ryals Lee, Jr., except: Victah Sailer (page 27)

ILLUSTRATIONS:
Craig Werkheiser, Kingfish Studio (page 11)

EDITORIAL SERVICES: Janice L. Smith for Penworthy

Library of Congress Cataloging-in-Publication Data

Hughes, Morgan, 1957-
    Track and field / Morgan E. Hughes.
       p. cm.
    Include indexes.
    Contents: [1] An Introduction to Track & Field — [2] The sprints — [3] Middle and long distance runs — [4] The jumps — [5] The throws — [6] Training and fitness.
       ISBN 1-57103-288-6 (v. 1). — ISBN 1-57103-291-6 (v. 2). — ISBN 1-57103-289-4 (v. 3). — ISBN 1-57103-290-8 (v. 4). — ISBN 1-57103-292-4 (v. 5). — ISBN 1-57103-293-2 (v. 6)
    1. Track-athletics Juvenile literature. [1. Track and field.] I. Title.
GV1060.5.H833 1999
796.42—dc21   99-20284
                                                                                        CIP

Printed in the USA

TABLE OF CONTENTS

Shot-putting requires strength and balance.

CHAPTER ONE

THE SHOT PUT

The sport of shot-putting may be one of the oldest known to man. Some historians claim that it is more than 2,500 years old. In American track and field programs, the shot put is probably the most popular weight event contested. It is an event for men and women, boys and girls, and is included even for the youngest (Bantam) athletes, age 10 and younger.

No matter who you are, how big or small, how old or young, you can participate in this exciting test of strength, balance, and technique.

The Basics

Like all track and field events, the shot put has some unique features. The shot itself is a ball made of steel or other metal. At the beginning level, Bantam athletes use a 4-pound (1.8-kilogram) shot. The weight of the shot gradually increases. Competitors at the Midget level move up to a 6-pound (2.7 kilograms) shot. In junior high school meets, an 8-pound (3.6 kilograms) shot is used. In high school the shot weighs 12 pounds (5.4 kilograms). In collegiate and Olympic competition the weight reaches 16 pounds (7.3 kilograms).

In addition to the shot, this event includes a specific launching, or **throwing circle** seven feet (2.1 meters) in diameter. The circumference (or outer circular edge) is marked by a band of metal, wood, or plastic which is raised no more than 3⁄4-inch (about 2 centimeters) above the surface of the circle itself. A **toe stop board** is secured to the outer edge of the circle to help the athlete plant for the release.

The shot-putter must remain inside the circle during the duration of the attempt. If the athlete steps out at any time during the delivery of the shot, the throw will be disqualified.

★ **DID YOU KNOW?**

Experts believe shot-putting (once known as "weight putting") was invented by the Celts of Scotland and Ireland around 500 B.C.

The shot-putter starts with her back to the target zone.

The balanced crouch puts the thrower's weight beneath the shot.

The Initial Stance

After you have found the most comfortable hand position, which you can determine by tossing the shot back and forth from one hand to the other, you're ready to take your initial stance. You may hold the shot under your ear and against your neck, or against your collarbone, depending on which is more comfortable.

To begin, stand at the rear of the circle (furthest from the **target zone** into which you will **"put"** the shot) with your back to the target. A right-handed putter will have his right foot furthest from the target. Stand relaxed and erect.

The Balanced Crouch

Balance is the most crucial element of shot-putting. Your shift across the circle begins when you lower your head and bend at the waist until your back is parallel to the ground.

The Glide Step

Keeping your hop, or **glide step**, very low to the ground, and the back leg extended for balance, you will begin your approach to release. The foot of your balance leg (your left leg if you are right-handed) will eventually be the one that plants against the toe stop board as you begin to rotate your body.

★ DID YOU KNOW?

American shot-putter Randy Barnes, winner of the 1996 Olympic gold medal, holds the world record at 75 feet, 10 inches (about 23 meters).

Your left arm, which starts out pointing away from the target zone, will swing around and help you build momentum and force for the release.

At the moment of release you want to have all your weight behind the shot so that you can explode upward and outward with maximum strength, launching the metal ball into the air toward the target.

A final explosion of energy occurs at the moment of release.

The shot-putter must remain in the throwing circle for the duration of
the attempt.

The Delivery and Follow-through

The delivery is made up of three moves: the lift, the pivot, and the push or put. At the lift, your weight is under the shot, with your left foot against the toe stop board and your right elbow directly behind you. In the pivot, your weight shifts to the front leg and your trunk (or torso) rotates forward.

The push or put action is the explosive release of strength when you let go of the shot. Your left leg will be straight as your weight continues to shift forward.

In the follow-through, you must reverse feet just after you release the shot, half-hopping to your right foot. This shift in weight allows you to maintain balance and avoid stepping out of the circle.

CHAPTER TWO

THE DISCUS

In the time of the ancient Greeks, the discus champion was often viewed as the greatest of all athletes. Even today, the discus thrower is the very symbol of track and field.

The object of this graceful event is to hurl the discus as far as possible while staying within a **throwing circle** that measures 8 feet, 2½ inches (2.5 meters) in diameter. It is an event for boys and girls starting at the Midget class (11 years and older).

Like many events, this one requires a combination of strength, grace, and balance—and, of course, technique.

The discus looks like a dinner plate with a tapered outer edge and comes in a variety of sizes and weights. Beginners will start out with a discus in the 3-pound (1.3-kilogram) range and gradually move up. At the college and Olympic level, the discus weighs 4 pounds, 6 ½ ounces (about 2 kilograms) and is approximately 8 ½ inches (about 22 centimeters) in diameter.

Some experts believe that taller athletes (with larger hands) may be more successful in this event, but no beginner should be discouraged from trying to master the discus throw. More than anything, hard work is the key factor.

The Grip and Delivery

Hold the discus in the palm of your throwing hand with your fingers curled slightly around the edge and your thumb across the surface of the discus for stability. As in the shot put, you will begin your approach to release from the rear of the circle.

DID YOU KNOW?

In ancient Greece, no athlete was more highly respected than the discus thrower, not even the heroic marathon runner.

The discus grip may be more easily mastered by athletes with
large hands.

During the windup, weight shifts off the back leg.

There are several kinds of deliveries, including the standing throw, and the spin and throw (which is the most advanced technique and the most difficult to master).

The Standing Throw

When you work up to the most difficult delivery method, you will execute one-and-a-half turns in the throwing circle before you release the discus for its high, flat flight path.

As a beginner, however, you should first learn the standing, or stationary, throw. To gain the right position, stand with your left foot at the front of the circle with your body sideways to the direction you'll throw the discus. Your feet should be shoulders-width apart, with your right foot near the center of the circle.

When you have the discus in a comfortable grip, with the first joint of your fingers overlapping the edge, swing it back and forth to establish a rhythm. As you bring the discus forward for release, begin to push off your right foot while straightening your left leg, and rotate your hips toward the target area. The hips must lead the throwing arm.

Your right arm should swing around in an upward plane. Release the discus at shoulder height, remembering to follow through in a smooth, controlled way to maintain your footing and balance.

> ★ **DID YOU KNOW?**
>
> Between 1976 and 1992, the Olympic discus gold medal went to German (or East German) women four out of six times.

The Turning (Spinning) Release

Discus throwers who are comfortable with their delivery may want to add a turn or spin to their release move. The turn is designed to help the thrower gain momentum (energy) which is transferred to the discus upon release. (This is the same purpose that the glide step serves in the shot put.)

The body opens up as the discus is released at shoulder height.

On release, the hips turn and weight shifts forward.

Stand at the back of the circle with your back to the target zone. Your feet should be shoulders-width apart and your weight should be on the balls of your feet. Swing the discus back and forth, then begin to turn your body slowly, speeding up as you reach the release point.

The throw begins with your weight on your right foot. As your left arm swings around, your weight shifts to your left foot and you pivot on it. Swing your right leg around, hop to the ball of your foot and pivot once. Now you're facing the target zone again and ready to release. Again, make sure the legs and hips are leading the throwing arm.

Follow-through and Balance

On release, your left arm swings around and your body opens up as you release the discus at shoulder height for a long, flat path through the air. Then, just as you did in the shot put, you must shift your weight from the left (throwing) foot to the right (follow-through) foot. This move, called a **reverse**, will keep you from spinning out of the throwing circle.

While strength is an important part of successful discus throwing, technique is even more important. Most coaches agree that working on the individual steps (the spin, the weight shifts) will accomplish more than bulking up. No matter how much strength you have, your throws will not be competitive if you don't have the correct technique.

CHAPTER THREE

THE JAVELIN

The **javelin** is another event that comes from the natural evolution of mankind. As hunters we began by using spears to bring down game.

The javelin can be one of the most exciting events in all of track and field. However, because of the design of the javelin itself and the unpredictable nature of even the best athletes, it may also be one of the most dangerous events.

In recent years, the javelin has enjoyed a growth in popularity among young athletes, and Youth class track athletes (age 13 and up) are now competing in this event.

There may be some advantages to the tall, slender athlete in this event, although a former world record holder from Finland, Jorma Kinnunen, threw the javelin more than 300 feet (90 meters) even though he stood only 5' 6" (1.65 meters).

Three different grips used in the javelin are the American, the Finnish, and the Hungarian. The most popular is the **Finnish grip**, in which the javelin is held secure by the thumb and middle finger. The tip of the middle finger is positioned at the forward edge of the grip binding. The American grip uses thumb and index finger. The Hungarian uses thumb and middle finger with the index finger extended straight along the length of the javelin. This puts great pressure on the finger upon release.

As a beginner, you will probably learn the Finnish grip so you can take advantage of the strength in your middle finger. Later, you may adopt your own grip.

★ DID YOU KNOW?

In 1952, with a throw of 242 feet, 1 inch (72.6 meters), Cy Young became the first American man to win the Olympic gold medal in javelin. No U.S. athlete has since earned the honor.

Concentration and consistency are important in events such as the javelin throw.

The javelin is carried above the shoulder during the approach run.

The Carriage/Approach

There are three different styles of approach carry: one in which the javelin is carried above the shoulder and pointed slightly upward, a second in which the javelin is carried above the shoulder and pointed slightly downward, and a third in which the javelin is carried low, with the throwing arm back and down. The first method is the most popular.

By carrying the javelin high and pointed slightly upward, you have a better chance to concentrate on technique because the spear is already in launch position. The carry is used during the first 60 to 80 percent of the approach distance.

The final stage of the approach run may be one of four styles: the hop-step, the rear cross-step, the front cross-step, or the combination hop and front cross-step. Any style of footwork that allows the thrower to gather momentum while maintaining full balance and control is acceptable.

The approach **runway** is four meters wide and has a scratch, or **foul line**, at the end. If you step over the line the throw is disqualified. Your approach may be up to 16 steps, with the release being made off the foot opposite your throwing hand.

Release Position

As you reach the end of your approach and take your two to four crossover steps, remember that you will "dig in" or "plant" with your left foot if you are a right-handed thrower, so your right heel will lead the final crossover step.

As you plant, your right shoulder moves back and the javelin is tipped back to a near vertical position. As your left foot strides and plants, your right arm draws back. With your chest up and head slightly to the left, point your left foot in the direction of the throw and bring your right elbow high over your head. Make sure that the hip turn leads the motion.

Performing a series of crossover steps helps the thrower gain momentum.

The right-handed athlete will plant his left foot when releasing
the javelin.

Follow-through and Reverse

As the javelin leaves your hand, snap your wrist for the final whipping action that will add length to the throw. You don't throw a javelin as you would a baseball or a football. Rather, you whip it through the air.

After release, you will use the same hop and reverse step used by shot putters and discus hurlers. This will keep you from losing your balance and stepping over the foul line.

Remember not to hold the javelin too tightly. Also, make sure that your elbow leads on the release and don't point the javelin too high when you turn it loose.

CHAPTER FOUR

THE HAMMER

Because of the great physical strength, coordination, and balance needed for this demanding event, the **hammer** throw usually is not included in track and field competitions for athletes younger than college age. Women have begun to throw the hammer only in the last few years.

The hammer throw rivals the shot put and discus throw as one of the most exciting events and one of the oldest sporting contests known to mankind, beginning in Scotland around 2,500 years ago.

Its name comes from the fact that early competitions actually featured a sledgehammer as the implement hurled for greatest distance.

The Hammer

The object itself has changed dramatically since it was first used in competition 25 centuries ago. The "hammer" now consists of a heavy steel ball at the end of a length of steel wire connected to a grip also made of metal.

The ball is approximately four inches in diameter and comes in various weights. Where high school programs offer the hammer throw, the weight for competition stands at 12 pounds (5.4 kilograms). The college and Olympic men's hammers have steel balls that weigh 16 pounds (7.3 kilograms).

The four-foot-long (1.2-meter-long) wire connecting the ball to the grip is known as the handle.

 **DID YOU KNOW?**

American John Flanagan won the 1900 Olympic gold medal with a hammer throw of 163' 1" (49.7 meters). In 1986, Russia's Yuri Syedikh set the world record at 284' 7" (86.7 meters).

The hammer used today bears little resemblance to the object first used in competition.

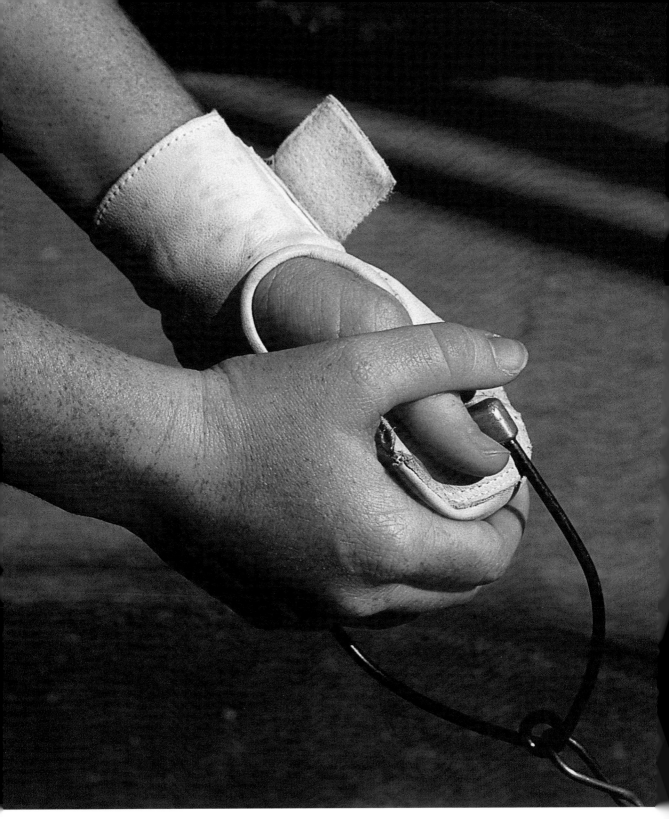

Protective gloves may be worn to protect the athlete's hands.

Just like shot putters and discus throwers, the hammer thrower is required to remain within a seven-foot (2.1-meter) circle for the duration of the attempt. Protective gloves are permitted as the friction of the handle rubbing against the palms of the athlete's hands can be very painful and damaging until proper calluses build up.

The Windup and Approach

Proper technique for a hammer thrower is very important, just as it is for all other throwing events. The strongest muscles are of no use if technique is not on an equal par. Only practice and a detailed understanding of the different parts of the windup and spin will allow beginning hammer throwers to achieve their goals.

Standing at the back of the throwing circle (just as shot put and discus throwers do), hammer throwers begin with their backs to the target zone. (The target zone is an area between two lines that extend at a 45-degree angle from the center of the circle, just as it is for the discus.)

The hammer thrower is not allowed to step out of the circle or even to step on the painted line that forms the ring itself. To make things even more difficult, there is no toe stop board, as there is in the shot put, to assist the throwers when they try to stop their forward momentum. As in all other throws, distance is measured from the edge of the ring to the landing spot.

> ★ **DID YOU KNOW?**
>
> The former East German standards for 13-year-old hammer throwers called for athletes to stand at least 5' 7" (1.7 meters), weigh 121-137 pounds (54-62 kilograms), and have an arm span at least 2 inches (5 centimeters) more than their height.

The Grip

When the thrower takes hold of his hammer, he will lay the handle across the fingers of his stronger hand (the right hand if he is right-handed). The left hand will go over the right hand, covering it. The grip should not be too tight. As always, it's important to relax.

Women did not compete in the hammer throw until recently.

The thrower must be careful to remain in the throwing circle after releasing the hammer.

Wearing leather-palmed gloves will protect the hands and keep any perspiration from affecting the grip (and thus affecting the throw itself).

This event requires great strength, but just as important are speed and balance.

The Throw

From a standing position at the rear of the ring, the thrower's back is to the target zone, with knees bent slightly and torso twisted slightly to the right. The ball itself is on the ground behind the thrower while the four-foot (1.2-meter) length of wire extends to the right. The left arm forms a straight line from the shoulder to the ball.

The thrower pulls the hammer off the ground in an upward sweeping motion, arms and body rotating. By making the hammer's low point in the orbit as far to the right as possible, the high point will then be at the release position, toward the target.

After three sweeps, the footwork begins. In a series of quick crossover steps and spins, the thrower comes to the front of the ring and releases, using the reverse technique of javelin, shot, and discus throwers to avoid stepping out of the circle.

CHAPTER FIVE

TRAINING TIPS FOR THROWS

Young athletes in the Bantam, Midget, Youth, Intermediate, and Young Adult age classes will have many opportunities to improve their skills at each of these difficult events (except the hammer throw, which comes later).

Along the way, there are many helpful tips that, if included in the daily training routine, can speed up the improvement and growth of the athlete.

Each event (shot put, discus, and javelin) has special and unique training tips. In addition, there are some tips which may be employed by athletes regardless of their event.

The Shot Put

You might be surprised to hear that many coaches recommend **jogging** as an excellent **warm-up** for shot-putters. You should also plan a series of bending and stretching exercises that will prepare the muscles in your back, neck, and shoulders.

To help develop technique, you should spend time putting or "punching" the shot from the front of the circle, without any steps or approach turns. Also, starting in the low crouch, practice the long stride backward and turn, with or without the shot. Concentrate on completing the foot, leg, and hip action before accelerating the upper torso.

You should spend time practicing the shift from the rear of the ring to the middle and finally to the front. This will enable you to develop balance, muscle memory, and confidence. During these sessions, concentrate on developing good rhythm and steady pacing.

★ DID YOU KNOW?

Although the shot put looks like an "arm strength" event, successful shot-putting actually gets 50% of all strength from the legs, 30% from the trunk, and just 20% from the arms.

Practice the release without taking any approach steps.

The mechanics—or technique—of discus are difficult to master.

As young throwers reach high school age, strength training becomes the dominant training regiment. Conditioning and stamina are also important, however, so don't be surprised if your coach has you run wind sprints as well as distances up to 200 meters at a time, with repetitions.

Discus

Start with some easy jogging to get your blood pumping and your heart rate up. Like any athlete, you must remember to take time to stretch. The few extra minutes you spend stretching at the start of a workout can save you weeks of inactivity if you seriously pull a muscle or tendon because you did not prepare properly.

Discus throwers must spend long hours working on mechanics. This means practicing the important turning component of the approach-to-release. This can be done in slow motion without the discus, and in stop-action, step by step, with the discus in hand.

★ **COACH'S CORNER**

Strength is vital in the discus. Some weight training lifts for discus throwers include (1) squats, (2) snatches, (3) cleans, (4) dead lifts, and (5) bench presses.

After you learn how to perform the turn and delivery, it is very important that you work on keeping your motion fluid. This comes only with repetitions and careful attention to the details of each segment. Your coaches will point out any flaws, but you must learn to be aware of when it doesn't feel right. Cheating or taking short cuts will only hurt your performance later when it really counts—in competition.

A javelin thrower must have strong legs as well as a strong arm.

Arm presses are a good idea for discus and shot put athletes.

Javelin

Upper body conditioning is vital for the successful javelin competitor. You can train with small weights (only with supervision) to build arm, shoulder, and chest muscles.

You should also spend lots of time running through repetitions of your approach, including the tricky crossover steps. By working out any of the kinks or unsteady aspects of your carry and approach, you will be able to concentrate on preparing for the proper release.

Repeat the carefully designed approach pattern until you can do it without thinking twice. Then you can worry about holding the javelin in the proper upright position and releasing it correctly.

Building Strength in Your Arms and Wrists

Cut a 16-inch (40-centimeter) length of broomstick, drill a hole carefully through the middle, then tie on a five-pound (2.3-kilogram) weight with a length of cord. Holding the broomstick at arm's length, roll up and unroll the cord with the weight and see how fast you feel your muscles "burn."

Strengthening Your Grip

You can dramatically increase the strength of your grip by spending some time each day squeezing a simple rubber ball (a tennis ball works well). Squeeze 50 times with one hand, then switch to the other. Continue to alternate hands. You can do this at night while you're watching your favorite TV show.

GLOSSARY

Finnish grip (FIN ish GRIP) — the most popular of the three main styles of holding the javelin, using the thumb and middle finger as primary clamps rather than thumb and index finger

foul line (FOUL LIN) — a line at the end of the runway in the javelin event over which the athlete may not step without having the attempt disqualified; also called the scratch line

glide step (GLID STEP) — part of the approach technique in the shot put that helps the athlete move from the rear of the throwing circle to the front edge for release

hammer (HAM er) — a throwing event featuring a 12- or 16-pound (5.4- or 7.3-kilogram) metal ball attached to a metal handle by a 4-foot (1.2 meter) length of steel wire (this event is not currently available to youth athletes)

javelin (JAV uh lun) — a spear-like apparatus 8 feet, 6¾ inches (2.6 meters) in length and weighing not less than one pound, 12¼ ounces (800 grams) (length and weight vary for men, women and youth athletes)

jogging (JAWG ing) — running at a slower rate of speed, used for warm-up sessions

put (POOT) — to propel the shot in the shot put event by extending the arm back, then straightening it so the shot is thrust into the air from the shoulder

GLOSSARY

reverse (ri VERS) — in all throwing events, this is the follow-through hop-step in which the weight of the athlete is transferred from the forward leg to the trailing leg to prevent stepping out of the throwing ring

runway (RUN WAY) — a long strip in such events as javelin, long jump, pole vault, which athletes use as an approach

throwing circle (THRO ing SER kl) — in the shot put, hammer, and discus throw, a circular area within which the athlete must remain during the entire throwing attempt

target zone (TAHR get ZON) — the area between two lines extending out from the center of the throwing circle at a 40-to-45-degree angle, into which the discus or hammer must be thrown to qualify for measurement

toe stop board (TO STAHP BAWRD) — a curved board, four inches (10 centimeters) in height, secured to the front of the throwing circle in the shot put event to help competitors avoid stepping out of the ring and thus being disqualified

warm-up (WAHRM UP) — a period of activity before an official workout or competition during which athletes gradually bring their body temperature up and stretch muscles to improve flexibility and comfort

FURTHER READING

Find out more with these helpful books and information sites:

Bowerman, William J. and Freeman, William H. *High Performance Training for Track and Field,* Human Kinetics, 1990

Carr, Gerry A. *Fundamentals of Track and Field,* Human Kinetics, 1991

Koch, Edward R. *USA Track and Field Directory,* USATF, 1993

Santos, Jim and Shannon, Ken. *Sports Illustrated Track: Field Events,* S.I., 1991

American Track and Field Online at www.runningnetwork.com/aft/

M-F Athletic Company at www.mfathletic.com (an online catalog for track and field books, tapes, clothes, etc.)

Track and Field News at www.trackandfieldnews.com/

United States of America Track and Field at www.usatf.org

INDEX